WESTERN MOTEL

WESTERN MOTEL

Poems by Wendy Drexler

Wendy Drexler

Turning Point

For Patricia,

What a pleasure to share
our poems in Provincetown —
with warmest wishes and
finding those sparks

August 22, 2014
Fine Arts Work Center

Published by Turning Point
P.O. Box 541106
Cincinnati, OH 45254-1106

ISBN: 9781936370702
LCCN: 2012935496

Poetry Editor: Kevin Walzer
Business Editor: Lori Jareo

Visit us on the web at www.turningpointbooks.com

Cover image: Edward Hopper, *Western Motel,* Yale University Art Gallery, bequest of Stephen Carlton Clark, B.A. 1903

Author photo by Debi Milligan

ACKNOWLEDGMENTS

I am grateful to the following publications in which these poems first appeared, some under different titles, some in different forms:

American Journal of Nursing: "Mile-High Home for the Aged"
Barrow Street: "America Earhart"
Brooklyn Review: "Son"
Cider Press Review: "Janis Joplin at Monterey" and "American Detritus"
Coin Flip Shuffle: "Then Let Us Be as Swimmers"
HeartLodge: "Western Motel" and "A Million Swainson's Thrushes"
Ibbetson Street: "Voodoo Donuts," "Deluxe Town Diner," and "The Unbuilt Prairie"
Meatpaper: "Diagram of a Cow in *Webster's* Tenth Edition"
Nimrod: "In the Kitchen"
Passager: "The City of the Cruise Ship *Valor*"
Penn Review: "Sunday River," "Man on a Wire," and "Uncertainty"
Peregrine: "Riding Bareback" and "The Book of Birds"
Off the Coast: "I'm Reading to Myself Again, Apollinaire," "Rooms by the Sea," and "Poem in Winter"
Poetry East: "When I Could Eat Again"
Pudding: "Parking Lot" and "Sunday Morning Bowling League"
RHINO: "Jewish Cemetery in Würzburg, Germany"
Sanctuary, the Journal of the Massachusetts Audubon Society: "Skunk Cabbage"
Tar River Poetry: "Salmon Run"
The Comstock Review: "Daughter," "Everything Makes Do," and "Two Horses in a Field"

"In the Kitchen" appeared in the anthology *Blood to Remember: American Poets on the Holocaust,* revised second edition, edited by Charles Adés Fishman, Time Being Books, © 2007.

"The City of the Cruise Ship *Valor*" appeared in *Burning Bright: Passager Celebrates 21 Years,* edited by Mary Azrael and Kendra Lopelke, Passager Books, © 2011.

"The Colorado River" appeared in *Rough Places Plain: Poems of the Mountains,* edited by Margot Wizansky, Salt Marsh Pottery Press, © 2005.

"Gas Stations, Drive-Ins, the Bright Motels," first appeared as a chapbook by the same title, Pudding House, © 2007 by Wendy Drexler.

With love and gratitude to my children, Julia Price Baron and Noah Baron; my loving husband, Herbert D. Friedman, who has supported me in all ways; Barbara Helfgott Hyett, for friendship, counsel, and magic; Suzanne Berger, for friendship and close reading of my manuscript; Debi Milligan, for friendship and photos; Mariève Rugo, for friendship and encouragement; Marie Howe and the nine sister poets at the 2011 Fine Arts Work Center in Provincetown; and all the members of the Workshop for Publishing Poets in Brookline, Massachusetts, where many of these poems were born, lost their moorings, and were born again.

Contents

I

Janis Joplin at Monterey.................................13

The City of the Cruise Ship *Valor*.....................14

Salmon Run..15

Voodoo Donuts...16

Diagram of a Cow in *Webster's* Tenth Edition...........17

Unemployment..18

Parking Lot...20

Bolt Bus..21

Sunday River..22

Mile-High Home for the Aged.............................23

America Earhart...24

Everything Makes Do.....................................25

The Unbuilt Prairie.....................................27

Sunday Morning Bowling League...........................28

Deluxe Town Diner...................................... 29

Special Olympics at the Harvard Track...................30

Consolation...31

Hawk..32

Counting the Bluebird's Eggs............................33

Man on a Wire...34

American Detritus.......................................35

II

Gas Stations, Drive-Ins, the Bright Motels..............39

III

Hopper's Landscape......................................57

What Distance Brings....................................61

Sky Study...63

White Palace..64

Marriage...65

Self-Portrait...67

The Book of Birds...68

Son...70

Daughter..71

Even Now...72

Poem in Winter..73

Skunk Cabbage...74

The Odds..75

When I Could Eat Again..76

Spider on the Music Stand..77

Two Horses in a Field 78

Then Let Us Be as Swimmers......................................79

Uncertainty...80

I'm Reading to Myself Again, Apollinaire.....................81

In the Kitchen...82

Jewish Cemetery in Würzburg, Germany 83

A Million Swainson's Thrushes 84

The Colorado River...85

Riding Bareback..86

What I wanted to do was to paint sunlight on the side of a house.

—Edward Hopper

I

JANIS JOPLIN AT MONTEREY

Hoarse with it, coarse with it,

        the shrill trills and come-on cries,

no slaking that voice, that thirst a saber

      of thistles and pearl,

        that American way of making it

    all up, severing the tyranny

       of home ties, peacocking,

          packed tight in gold lamé
like gunpowder,

        her colonies rebellious, and all

      embargoed cargo   dumped

        from the dock.

THE CITY OF THE CRUISE SHIP *VALOR*

I am a little god on vacation, entitled
to gamble five nights in the Shogun Casino
among brocade samurai and slot machines,
the bell-ringing bets, the humanly frivolous
cries. I overeat at the midnight dessert
buffet beneath the tiled wall mural of Rosie
the Riveter. I spend hours steeping
in the whirlpool, arrange my pedicure,
my aroma-spa ocean wrap. Someone
changes my linens, scrubs my toilet.
Someone brings me piña coladas while I sun
beside the pool, flashing my tattoo
and my gold chain. I bought perfume
and a leather wallet from the poor
in every port, and paid good money
to kiss a dolphin. And if I buy the skin
of the last blue iguana from a boy
who follows me from stall to stall
like a dog? Am I not from the City
of the Ship? And if I'm seasick, I call
my room steward to bring me Dramamine.
She turns down my sheets, folds my towels
into snakes on my bed—black dots
where eyes should be. Forgive me.

SALMON RUN

It is always life or death—Chinook, Coho, Sockeye
    inching, first stair-step up the ladder,
        and the woman sits and clicks

each one past the underwater glass window—
    salmon thrum, salmon clobber, singular,
        desperate by ones, by twos, salmon

sling themselves, fling themselves, fall back
    by fives, by tens. In this way, they meter out
        life's dry measure—ghosts lost

in the spillway, sucked into the turbines,
    shredded by the intake grates by twenty,
        by one hundred, roiled downriver

in the tailrace by one thousand, diminished,
    three thousand and five, three thousand
        and four, diminishing, three thousand

and three
    savaged mad
        with singing.

VOODOO DONUTS

—Portland, Oregon

Voodoo Donuts is
open all night and the guy at the
counter reads my name tag from the
party at the Chinese Garden, says his name
is Drexler, too.   So on his say-so I
order an Oreo   peanut donut
and we talk   about how
Drexler   means wood
turner in   German, how
we might   be related.
Every day   a new chip
flies off the   lathe at the
donut shop,   you just don't
know what will   happen. Life
stands in the middle of the donut hole, and
the Dragon Dancers at the party who
took off their masks were just
schoolboys and girls,
ordinary, shy.

DIAGRAM OF A COW IN *WEBSTER'S* TENTH EDITION

The nimbus of numbers radiating from (1) to (38),
pointing like stakes, oh, steaks, no mistaking (5)
the ribs; (8) barrel, that hippodrome; (19) the neck.
The butcher's cuts: (30) brisket; (37) tough rump;
(38) tender loin. Endearing horsey names: (24)
muzzle, velvety plateau and its abide with me;
(17) withers, the gently whither shall we and away we;
(4) switch; (9) the horsefly's buzz. Heart girth, (18)
the bulging bled to the highest bidder. How the cow's
all profile, the head, (37) three-quarter view,
considered by the (149) artists of the floating world
to be the most beautiful, revealing and concealing
(16) the crops, (5) the hocks
in hock, the have-nots filched, parsed,
bred for it, fed for it, dead for it.

UNEMPLOYMENT

Persistence 5, Tenacity 10
—Poster on the office wall

It's 8:08, I'm twenty-
third in line, waiting
for 8:30, opening
time. Someone hands
me a clipboard form
to sign my name,
my social, and we
are sent to sit side
by side on green
foam chairs. We are
laid off, off-course,
outsourced, all of us
cast up like rainbow
trout, red-capped or
blue, Birkenstocked,
tattooed, texting or
staring or reading
the weekly *Phoenix,*
scrim of hope. After
this, we can take a
workshop to interview
with power, critique
a résumé, consider
maturity vs. age.

I'm three weeks out,
the writs of work
fade away—file
names, lunch mates,
watch list, paycheck,
pride. I must be my
own second cup
of coffee, strong.

PARKING LOT

Cyclone fence, the daylight spill
of grocery bags casually snagged

empty on the bare corset of a branch.
I look out at the weak light of November.

A starling on the Norway maple
in the parking lot shakes

itself out all over, spangle-singing
into the wind's wide mouth.

I eat a bacon cheeseburger in the car.

BOLT BUS

Outside the wide, wide window,
slurry of greywoodsky

a little blue. I, too, am, too,
and subject to revision, patching

potholes in my storyline.
I'm retired, I say to the office

parks through mirror glass.
How expansive, bare trees of winter!

Traffic rustles past as the Bolt
bumps on the black canals of highway.

I'm a fish thrashing in a bucket
of daylight. My life is moving

faster than my life.

SUNDAY RIVER

—Our friend shuffles, unsteady
on the patio, weightless as a paper doll.
He comes to sit among us, occupied
with small motions of cutting and eating.
Talk swirls around him,
a revolving door he can't enter.
Tell us, I ask, *what have you loved?*
He grapples to strap
consonant to vowel to name
the mountain he loved to ski—
We wait on the other side
of the terrible silence that keeps him
from us. At last he remembers,
Sunday River, his voice rising assertive,
and aren't we grateful then, released
from our dread—vacancy and ravagement—
schussing and swiveling and clinging
to him down that deep white swath.

im Barclay Adams

MILE-HIGH HOME FOR THE AGED

For lunch they wear clean white shirts,
Brooks Brothers jackets, everyone's hair
smoothed back. Nurses wheel them in
so we can sing "O Beautiful" for them.

Someone sips his water, puts it down.
Someone can't stop scratching.
Has he lost his ballpoint pen?

Someone is wiping eye crust
from his brow's fruited plain.

Cracked alabaster toenails gleam. Let them all
clap the offbeat's spacious skies
as long as they like.

Let them sing loud majesty, off key,
or whispered, disconcertingly *bel canto,*
voices flocking like swallows, shedding
their grace on me.

AMERICA EARHART

And didn't she shimmy into
the last leg of that last flight to cast herself
into the all-metal that would

free her—gilded cage
of marriage, publicity, the Depression,
the Lindy girl clamping down like a lid on a pot,

outlandish siege and triumph,
ice on wings, gasoline dripping, no

flare, no Morse Code key, no parachute,
life jacket, dangling
radio antenna, drift, the moon riveted
to its rough hide,

all the gravelly stars, Africa,
its broad forest, the swath never to be

found in, every brave
and shimmering slick of sea for easy entry.

EVERYTHING MAKES DO

The farmer calls his goats his *lovelies,*
his *sweet things,* says he gave up

half his insides to cancer. Now he wraps
his life around his wife as tightly

as knotted socks in a drawer. Someday
he's going to build her a big kitchen.

He sells us a carton of eggs, carrots
clinging to their feathery tops.

Everything makes do with what it's got.
In those photos you took that day, wasn't

the farmer leaning against his rusted tractor,
and a cottonwood tree stripped of bark?

We drove past the tumult of peat bog,
worm casts, the bulwark of uncut timothy grass.

And weren't we fine? I still have the book
of *Twentieth-Century American Poetry*

you bought me for my birthday, inscribed
My Dearest. We lay on your bed, turned on

and reading Ferlinghetti, thinking we two
would tilt the world.

im Ronald Wohlauer

THE UNBUILT PRAIRIE

I used to roll down the top of my souped-up

    yellow Karmann Ghia, rev that engine

        through gears out Parker Road

    east of Denver just past the last

    sprawling ranch in its boxy plot,

nothing but fields—slant weed, sagebrush, dirt

        the color of a suede vest.

    The girl I was walked out there needing

    solid ground, the unpracticed

        blue-stacked Rockies, promised

only to themselves.

SUNDAY MORNING BOWLING LEAGUE

Shiny balls—marbled as meat—glide
down the alley's rumble right to the pocket—
thonk thonks, contained explosion.

No matter what happened yesterday
or what might come in the night,
they take their strikes, their spares,

seriously, anchored in camaraderie—
high-fives, the slapping of shoulders,
nice ball. Dark wings of sweat angle

under their arms. On their knit shirts,
the cursive letters of their names, intimate as silk,
hover blue above their hearts, every frame

of fallen pins risen again as the next man slips
into the ball's three-fingered glove,
his quiver of any sorrow briefly unslung.

DELUXE TOWN DINER

Refuge of the Dream—Gulden's
spicy brown on Hebrew National,
honey bear, bottle of Tabasco,

cartel of napkins, dispensed white
from steely towers, and the grill:
the short-order cook in his blue baseball cap

is humming hard work's Anthem.
One practical flick of the wrist
flips a pancake wide as a prairie.

Waitresses clatter plentiful platters—
black angus, tabouli and tofu, tongol tuna,
polyglot Reubens and Rachels, Cobb salad,

democratic potpies. All day
breakfast rides, like a good poem,
on its own melting, as Robert Frost says,

and all the yolks are sunny side. Deep in our duct-
taped booth, we are sated, flutter
greenbacks from our wallets, plenty of change.

SPECIAL OLYMPICS
AT THE HARVARD TRACK

Those who can walk, walk twice around—
        those who can run, run—or limp, twitch,
rock back and forth, shudder, mutter *no, never*—

and it's hot and hard to look at them and I can't
        decide—is it that they wear their nerves
on their faces, or how slight the skew when genes

fly out of bounds, or when too-little air
        at the surface short-circuits? And how
little is too little? A coach sprays sunscreen

on a boy who palms it into his skin, his smile
        unfenced as jazz. I cheer for our Victor,
whose tongue glides in and out, plowing

the track for gold, for number seven shuffling
        for bronze, and for the one who's come
in last and clamps tight hands over his ears in joy.

My heart runs hard in its cage.

CONSOLATION

And dead fish eyes set in silver
bezels, ringed and pouched and crumpled.
And the sun that made those eyes glisten,

or lit them from within. Smaller
than my thumb, knife-thin and rubbery.
No, not rubbery, exactly, but not yet stiff,

either, and still sweet-smelling. The skin,
immaculately foiled with cross-hatched
lines that scrolled all up and down.

And the mouth, two bronze shutters,
that tail, a gossamer, a ghost, a ship,
though all day I had been trying to renounce

metaphor. And wondered if Death
will make me beautiful, and hated
Death more for that irony—not to see

anything at all! And so my consolation
was less than I'd hoped for—only beauty
and death held together in my palm.

for Marie Howe

HAWK

Massive, implacable as a cannon,
      wings draped wide as tents.

He hunched over that squirrel
      staunched and pinned
brutal, to ground.

Delicate feathered feet,
      the fascicles contracting,
that smooth shiver.

He bent, plucked, reeled in
      the long thin red ribbons
of entrails, clamped down

on blood-slather, severed
      and separated dark

from light in the deepening dusk.

    Then he rose, tearing

        the air behind him.

COUNTING THE BLUEBIRD'S EGGS

Four eggs are blue as the best
new crayon in the box.
Inside the swell of shell, flesh
lounges down. Four beaks auger out,

chicks who'll carry sky on their backs,
hungry for a green caterpillar,
the skid-lines of the spine.
Seventeen days, or eighteen,

gray-blue subdued, a clockwork switch:
pinion, bone wheel into the broth
of air—no tears, no goodbye,
no lingering discourse or recourse,

no holding, no proof of stay,
only the empty nest—the stubble
snag-frazzled, red pine needles
crushed to nothing now.

MAN ON A WIRE

To mince into thinness, utterly absorbed, every

microcentimeter quivering the sovereign brace

and ballast of each slow muscle, each bushel of air.

To inflect the slack middle, swaying above dissonance.

To threshold the balancing pole like a bride across.

To let no one reach him, no one catch him, not even

the cops who come close: only the rake of light,

the ledge his refusing, taking his time.

To stay then, ecstatic like that—

AMERICAN DETRITUS

—Amtrak, Washington to Boston

Trees grow runty along the tracks
like the past itself—smokestacks, sheds
and chimney pots, broken backs
of buildings that stare back. Chipped brick walls,
rusty carny machinery, waist-high weeds, a sea
of sagging water towers, slag heaps, waves

of staved-in roofs. Cracked windows won't wave
back at graffiti-sprayed boxcars stuck on tracks.
The Schuylkill slithers, slinks to sea-
side factories slack with vines that shed
their blooms. Cyclone fences wall
off crumbled concrete. Trenton turns its back

on double-deckers, clapboard-bare, back-
yard-trash. Manhattan towers cast waves
of light on small shops closing shop, their walls
no longer stocked with made-in-America tracks
of worsted woolens, union-spun. The sheds
of tool-and-dye shops emptied of the sea-

green lathes, vise-grips, drill bits, the scrappy sea
that brought the immigrant stream from Ellis, back
from steerage, packed in bunk-bed rows, they shed

their lives, inched their way by day shift, waved
on the low-pay piecework, garment racks on tracks.
Whole factories bristle with decay—walls

where cutters, clothiers darkly toiled—walled
in hardship shadowing the coast, a sea
of smoke and fumes, torched, scorched, tracks
the whole earth clogged. Slathered backs
of choking marshes, oil slicks, poisoned waves
punked up with mercury. Watersheds

grown rife with loosestrife burn beneath the shed
of greenhouse sky that closes down to wall
time in, as now the train descends in waves
of smog, tilting north to shoreline and the sea.
Sunlight simmers through the backs
of clouds turned hard as tarnished pots. The Amtrak

thrums to Boston, tracks the past, which shed
its grace on labor's back, before the Wall
Street plunge, banknotes tumbling like waves at sea.

II

GAS STATIONS, DRIVE-INS, THE BRIGHT MOTELS

i.
Daffodils that sang of yellow,
saw only yellow, awoke

from the yellow other side.
Clouds clattered downward,

upward into vanished air.
I was a child, wobbling

the wet cement on my bike.
Already good

at cutting corners, how could I
not ride out this far?

ii.

Nothing has happened yet—
so I scratch a piece

of linoleum kitchen counter
with a paper clip to see

whether or not I'm sorry. Daddy
comes home. Mommy tells him

to spank me. He has never
spanked me. His voice rises,

then dies. Maybe he won't.
My life is a yellow box

too short for pencils. When
I play, I play alone: separate

into families my trading cards—
horses from flowers from birds.

I let my yo-yo sleep
on the end of the string, cut out

a new pink dress with sparkles
for my Wendy doll, take off

the plain paper dress she wears
around the house, press onto her

the tabs of her gown, wind up
the ballerina in the music box,

make her spin on one thin toe.

iii.
Mommy takes me to Denver
Dry Goods to buy me
buttons, one of every kind—

smooth ones, twin ones
with yellow stones or blue,
sparkling see-throughs with eyes,

a pearly one, a swirly one,
and six flat coat buttons stitched
to a card. At home, I let them

loose on my bed—the ladybug,
the fruit basket with its lipstick-
red apple, the cherry-pinks.

iv.
I pretend Mommy and Daddy
are married again, and I'm in
the orphanage—eating
meat loaf and peas, jiggling

Jell-O with my fork. I feed a spoonful
to my dolls—Penelope,
Pitiful Pearl, Ginger, who can cry.
Mommy and Daddy have come

to pick me out. For Mommy, I twirl
in my black-patent shoes.
The yellow tulips on my skirt
bow and sway. For Daddy, I smile.

Well, well, who have we here?
he asks. *I'm Wendy,* I say,
in Peter Pan. He hugs me,
tells me, *You're the one we want!*

v.
In our yellow kitchen, Mommy trims
the crusts, serves me my sandwich

on my plate, my glass of milk.
I rub my rabbit's foot for luck—

the fur, then the bone. After lunch,
she has me rinse my dish and glass,

put them in the GE's top rack.
Then she takes them out

to show me how to make them fit.

vi.
In his house, Daddy gives me a puzzle—
can I draw a man and a dog with only

three lines? I make one line for Daddy, one line
for Mommy, and one line for the magic door

Daddy's disappeared through. Mommy
has packed the wrong pajamas and there's no

night-light. I get up from the foldout couch,
turn on the yellow lamp to play jacks.

Starting with onesies, I toss that little ball.
Squeeze those steely stars until I bleed.

vii.
Saturdays, Daddy picks me up
from Mommy's to take a drive—

I beg him to roll down
the top of his Corvette, and he rolls

it down. I beg him to drive fast,
and he drives fast. At the House

of Pancakes, in our favorite booth
next to the window, I order

my three silver dollar pancakes
and one fried egg. I like to squish

the yellow with my fork. Watch it run.
On the paper placemat, I draw a house

with a crayon to practice
long division. I draw 12 x's in the house.

Daddy draws a garage next to
the house with three x's in it

so I can find out how many x's
from the garage fit inside the house.

All the x's belong to me. Daddy is
the trillion million everything

is divided into. Daddy's Corvette
does not live in our garage anymore.

viii.
I want my shoebox at home
in the closet with all my matchbooks

bound with rubber bands,
the one with the yellow cover

of the pizza shop, the one
from the drive-in, the ten gas stations,

every bright motel. I beg
Daddy to buy me cowgirl boots

with silver stars that always shine.
What can he do but drive

to buy them? On our way, I try
to count the Denver lights,

but there are too many. Headlights
push back the green fists of woods.

Daddy loves having me
all to himself. He palms

his hand around the gearshift,
slides it down. He's singing

Clementine. It's too dark
to read my comic book. I wonder

if the Earth spins out and back.
Does the moon have light of its own?

I turn my face away. Daddy takes me
to the Top Star Motel to stay the night.

May we have some matchbooks?
Daddy asks the man in the lobby.

I fish one out of the big glass bowl.
A riddle under the cover:

Why did the cowboy ride his horse?
Because the horse was too heavy to carry.

ix.
The mattress at the motel is perfect
for jumping. Daddy reads his paper
in the Naugahyde chair. He puts a quarter
into the Magic Fingers machine that shakes me
on the bed like a bumper-car ride.

Daddy is letting me bring for just a night
the kitten that Mommy won't let me keep.
I line a drawer with a bathroom towel
for the kitten. Daddy says, *Wendy's such
a good little mother.* I open

all the other drawers to see if anyone
has left something for me. The kitten
gets lost under the stiff drapes.
Daddy tucks both of us in, kisses
the kitten, kisses me. The neon sign

out the window yellows on and off
and the cars on Colfax won't hold
still. Daddy tells us *Cinderella*
in the dark. She was good and did
as she was told and never complained.

x.
I can do the basting stitch
from the *Brownie Scout Handbook*,
fold hospital corners on my bed.

Run like sheep, roll like tumbleweed,
jump into water over my head.
I know every planet by color,

Saturn's pat of butter, red Mars.
I know how oysters rest, how to be
that closed.

xi.
I'm mean to Mommy's boyfriends.
I sulk. One of them scowls,

I pity the man you'll marry.
I stare at Jack's limp

even though he gave me
a badminton set, stretched

the yellow net for me on the front lawn.
And when Norman, who sits

down beside me at the dinner
table, asks if he can

marry my mother, I shake
my head from side to side, flick

my braids like whips. I tell him
I want her to marry Jack.

After, Mommy says I can hate
Norman if I like, *just be polite.*

xii.
Dear Mommy,
Someone should have told you
before you left that my babysitter

Bookie is a lot of trouble.
She doesn't know where anything is.
There are a lot of things that you forgot

to tell her. What slip do I wear
with my party dress? On Halloween
Bookie couldn't put my freckles on.

Daddy gave me a new doll.
She has black hair and is one
of those rubber dolls that you can move.

He bought her for me in Mexico.
She has a white dress with gold on it.
Daddy says maybe he'll take me

to Mexico someday. Yesterday
the dog cut his hind foot on a nail
and he's a bloody mess.

I hope you and Jack are having
a nice time at your honeymoon.

xiii.
I hate the rodeo dust, though
the horses could be happy—
all the people watching them
under the lights in that big-
enough ring.

Leaning out too far, cowboys
twirl ropes to snap
the calves' legs
and bring them down.
Daddy buys me

a chameleon on a little leash
to pin on my sweater.
I look down and watch it
turn yellow and brown. If I let it,
how far could it go?

xiv.
Daddy takes Bobbi and me to ride
the roller coaster at Lakeside
three whole times because we are

so brave. After, Daddy gives us
a quarter to spin the dial
of the Scent O'Matic

in the Ladies' Room—
Je Reviens, L'Air du Temps,
Taboo—we press the plunger

and place our wrists
under the nozzle, spray *Taboo.*
Brush our bangs

into a gloss, retie our hair
with yellow rubber bands, swish
our ponytails the way

we want, practice smiles,
a pretty one for Bobbi,
a careful one for me.

xv.
Daddy brings me a Comprehensive
World-Wide Stamp Album where
every stamp belongs: Prince Rainier,

all his denominations, Hegel,
a soldier from Epirus, the Hungarian
factory worker. Daddy holds

the glassine bag. I slip out
the luna moth from Mozambique.
We turn the pages in my thick book.

I lick the gluey hinge, press that stamp
into place. We pour over heads of state—
Queen Elizabeth on Dominica's

one-cent shore, Prince Charles
guarding Fiji, emerald and yellow
neon parrots from Ecuador

who need only a stamp to be secure.

xvi.
Daddy is generous with his ladle
of small talk. At the Skyline Restaurant

he orders fries and hamburgers, rare,
for us, stops ginger ale inside his straw

for me, laces his fingers, makes
the church and the steeple

and all of the people come back,
balances the salt shaker

on a single grain of salt.
The waitress is a golden eagle

with my Shirley Temple on a tray.
I love the ice cubes floating

in my glass, promising
to stay. I'm hooked like a fish,

want any bait Daddy flings—
jokes, bracelets, a rainbow

of colored pipe cleaners
from the dime store,

the yellow roe of his affection,
intense as fiction. I need

that glittering flash and dazzle.
Daddy asks if I'm finished

with my bun, my leftover meat. I nod.
He takes it onto his plate to eat.

xvii.
At intermission at the drive-in,
I ask Daddy where babies come from.

He tells me the penis goes into
another hole that's not

for peeing. I have to see,
run to the ladies room, lock myself

into a stall, raise one leg on the toilet
to try. *Where* is it the baby comes out?

The bathroom lights flicker on and off
three times. The floodlights dim

pale yellow and the speakers crackle
tin again. I creep past the kissing couples

in their cars. I will never ask
my father *anything* again.

xviii.
I trace myself back into being,
that mouth, a purse snapped shut.

My braids are as tight as the rosebuds
in the smocking of my dress.

My puffed sleeves hold their breath.
We were three marigolds

in the window box—pinching back
our lavish blooms.

III

HOPPER'S LANDSCAPE

Rooms by the Sea

Slit of bedroom tightened

to hard seam—flank of dresser, carpet, couch—

our thirst, our fear. Who knows

what will happen? The sea quivers.

The sun's a white smear,

and the honeybees   are humming, drumming

like a truce the darkening dunes of sand.

If they tear a blossom—beach pea or goldenrod—

are they not done

with need, at least the heavy

end of need? How else

to live in this world?

Western Motel

Have I been sitting here for hours,
straight-backed on the bolstered bed,
alone among the molten elements,
sand ground down to its hardest part?
Hours jut and leer like a car's
chrome mouth. One last flare
of gold, and the hills gather into loaves.
To be the one. To be the only one,
my wrist shapely and disconsolate.
My fingers grip the bedrail hard.
I console myself with light detached
from the empty wall. If I let my hair
go wild, will shadows spill
their liquid spines, and break?
Everything is right
beyond my vision—prologue,
denouement, the ringing of the bells
after the bells have rung.

Gas

The pump jockey divides

the station from the pines'
dark gnarl. Each night
shutters the day before.

The three gas pumps retreat
to their patient domes,
the glow rimmed in, the flying

Mobilgas horse frozen mid-leap
in his icy neon sky. Everything
turned or turning, arching up.

The doorway is always. Blank
windows stare. Macadam

bends out of sight—no one
ever coming—only orange

roadside grasses to hold
back the regiment of woods.

Sun in an Empty Room

Don't call it *empty,* call it *waiting,*
if you are, and call it *vigilant* if you are.

Touch everywhere
before you walk in—

wood rustling, wind glittering—stretched taut across.

The floor is mustered. Green from trees
warms the sill.

A wedge whittled where wall meets wall.
Night is coming to the window. Let it

take the whole house into heartbreak, into halo.

WHAT DISTANCE BRINGS

Who knows why desire grows
        in its own shadow? We see

a distant lighthouse punctuating
        that sandy spit,

the sky swollen, rinsed in haze, swarming
        like a herd of stallions—

        we like to say that—
           a herd of stallions—

and when we get there, the lighthouse
        is a stack of white-chipped brick.

Don't all clouds obscure something
        we thought we wanted? It's distance

creates desire, and the lighthouse
        better far away. We want the singing—

gleam and shine, gleam and shine,
        which leaps from our hands, or is

too terrible. We want a frame
                       to contain the vastness.

             We want a Hopper postcard
      to hang on a wall. We want

to hold the sun but not
           its burning, or we want to burn.

SKY STUDY

—Light of clotted cream with recourse

to hills, two mares grazing, the hills ridged

and sweating from every pore,

the hills hollow

without regret

like two cloth napkins

shaken out on the table

heaped and pleated

accountable to the obbligato

of circumstance, committed

to brief stains and dissolution—

WHITE PALACE

. . . high in a white palace the king's daughter,
the golden girl . . .
          —F. Scott Fitzgerald

To be the princess, that kind of adoration.
Anyway, I wanted the terror, the smelter
of ambition, the desire burning through
the wick. To spin like a needle in a compass,
true north with longing. The kind of love
that tears pine trees out by the roots.
That kind of love. No going back.
The kind of love that never works out.

MARRIAGE

We divided it piece by piece, split
the knives, each with its own glittering

talent, split the rubble
of the kitchen drawer—

matches, birthday candles,
batteries, rubber bands.

The copper casserole, the pastry board,
home movies, you behind the camcorder,

consuming my attention. It was I
who chose Satie's *Gymnopédie*

for walking down the aisle, and for after,
a brisk bourrée. My mother chose

the wedding gown, dotted swiss.
Embroidered daisies. You wouldn't wear

the white shirt. She loathed
the Marimekko tie you'd sewn

yourself, your hippy hair,
Earth Day pin riding

the lapel of your raw silk suit.
I was the skittish bride, afraid to skip

to the front of the buffet line.
We sipped champagne, my lips

on your glass, your lips on my glass.
I swam toward the coves

of your eyes, meant to
anchor there.

SELF-PORTRAIT

I took off
my skin, tied

and untied
the satin lacings of my dress.

A painter's knife
anchored the rivulets of my lips.

My cheeks had nowhere
to hide. I was

precondition—a copy
of a copy: lover, mother.

Small, fallible martyr.

THE BOOK OF BIRDS

Let us match the bird in the bush
with the one in the book, find the name
of the one in the book in two languages.

The sparrows—*Melospiza melodia*—
at the boat pond in Central Park, the rafter
of their wings. The terns at Newcomb Hollow

rearranging themselves like sentences
over the sea that filled when it was empty.
The pigeons strutting like prizefighters

on an air conditioner at the back
of the Marriott. Preening, clicking
their toes. Each grooming the other

as delicately as a pastry above the traffic.
Birds are so unlikely—their nests, their instincts
in the grip of light, their seasons, the shape-

shifting gears of their feathers, their pair bonds,
their neurons pulsing without the impediments
of speech. Let me read to you again

of waxy red wings, the robin's
red breast. Let us match the one
in the bush with the one in your hands.

for Julia and Noah

SON

The lean stalk of him drinking there,
arch and length, rake and thrust
without boundary or reserve.

I could squash that needy hunger
with my hand, swoop down on him,
pull him away from what? Some
socket of harm? Some refusal?

The maddening sortie of his small
bold will? Poised between the ends
of things and what must yield,

I squeeze his arm too hard,
until he screams. A few
swollen seconds, then
everything is danger,
      falcon—
             sharp rib
and beak. I am
weak   with power.

DAUGHTER

Climbing Bearberry Hill, you ask me
the name of those wild pink roses

that stipple the dunes. I used to know.
Oh, thicken, memory. *Rosa rugosa.*

Remember this: *Ma mère* and I
in matching summer skirts and blouses,

I must have been five. And didn't I
twirl full circle twice, unfurled,

and and *and* and *and,* the tight
and trial from which I became.

And you, my girl, your sleep a cave
where dogs bark all night. You burn

fires there, paint lavender tigers
on your wall to follow you—

one for the doors of the dance
to swing open, one that sails out

on slow-moving water. The last is
for love, every day leaving, coming back—

EVEN NOW

And if
you ask,
even now,
my daughter,
I will
tell you,
Yes, I'm
sorry, from
the first
day we
told you
in the
dining room
it was
over. You
screamed and
yanked a
hank of
my hair.
I let
you. Even
now, I'd
let you.

POEM IN WINTER

We get by. Even
the icicled branches,
a porch rail's dabble,

boats too dark for detail.
Breakwater,
more water—
tide's wave fray,

a velvet-blue smear undoing
the horizon line, shuttling
back to find the next
best thing.

We will never be done
with beauty, the glass
of the world filled
with quietude—and all

the small creatures
who lie down gracefully,
gratefully under mud, in ice.

SKUNK CABBAGE

Out of nowhere, then,

    skunk cabbages astonish

        the meadow:

pursed and swollen spathes,

putrid fists, ugly, unreticent, and inside,

        a knotted yellow swarm.

Slugs, snails, five-lined skink,

    blue-bottled flies are avid

on the cud of mottled leaves

        whose stench is salvage.

How long winter slung itself

        over my shoulder,

each rogue thing

        obstinate, returning—

THE ODDS

Hello, I say. *Nice sweater,* he says. What odds and
oddities, what one-in-one thousand chance do we find
ourselves side by side in Memorial Hall, years after
our eight thousand nights? The musicians tune for
The Curse of the Rhinegold. He turns to tell me our old
joke: "The reason the Renaissance lasted so long was
it took all that time to tune the lutes." Do I smile, or
not, assemble my pose and repose, strain my thigh
away from his thigh, the hairs on his fingers? He
clears his throat, coughs. The swan-bone flute sounds
its hollow frequency. Every night I'd turn to him in
bed, drape my leg like a shawl over him, our oath
plied and sworn—*God, how I betrayed him.*

WHEN I COULD EAT AGAIN

That first small bite of toast
                was acres of wheat,
gold and clashing in wind.

And the spoonful of applesauce
          on my tongue was
                an orchard,
the bee's honey and the bee's sting.

The vase beside my bed
          held blossoms
                to pinkness,

each mindful of its own
          cut stem.

SPIDER ON THE MUSIC STAND

I'm playing Bach's Cantata 5, so vast
it seems to set those spinnerets to gleam:
Spider drapes the silken thread, reams
of beaded pleats, all the measured tasks.
The web's a limber snare, the fly caught fast.
Impact strums the serious air. Legs lean
on ladders—skitter down taut rungs, trapeze
the dragline. In a flurry, Spider clasps
and wraps the shrouds of swirling. Venom stuns.
Spider winds that fly in silk's death spin,
invested in the bloody win. Time's sum
acquits me, too, for things I've done. Come,
day, forgive my dance of will or whim,
stay, sweet music—spider dust and crumbs.

TWO HORSES IN A FIELD

The stallion strokes the engine
of his legs, barrel and buttocks

quivering in waves as he
stands behind the roan mare,

sniffs her fusty rump. Simple—
grazing in rain, their quiet,

their sustenance, their private
courtesies, his penis that sways

free as a bough in the fenced
pasture, sweet and calm—

no harness, no cart, nothing
foolish, no mistakes.

THEN LET US BE AS SWIMMERS

Then let us be as swimmers, sleek
in our own wet skin. I know

better than to bargain this time.
I amuse myself with damselflies,

ruby, flickering, basting the sky.
Dare I call you mine, bind you

to me, love you? My hands hold
nothing, hide nothing. My heart

must improvise a little—let love stretch
the sides of this poem, the way day

lilies climb spires, poured from sleep
or from a dream of sleep.

UNCERTAINTY

The roses you brought me
      are intimate, each petal
            untutored, tightly held,

curling in toward the bud
      of becoming, like
the still-clenched fist

of your heart. Could we love
      with such conviction? How
         unafraid

you say you are.

I'M READING TO MYSELF AGAIN,
APOLLINAIRE

I'm reading to myself again, Apollinaire—
as I look up from the poem, I see that you have
closed your hazel eyes and shrouded them
with a face cloth to keep my light from streaming in.

Your jaw is slack as you snore like a small city
beginning its day, trucks delivering the morning
news.

        Love is not the dice we have scattered,
but the place we have so providently landed—
I the metal thimble; you, the shoe. *I must be
careful when I compare us.*

In Paris, the poet walked the Seine, leaf staunch
and giveway, one tree fanning another, one tree
shading another as a reason for happiness.

IN THE KITCHEN

I am cutting a cucumber
and listening to a string quartet
on the radio written by the prisoners
of Theresienstadt. I peel
long green strokes in the name
of your grandfather, murdered
there, his life worth less than a sack
of wheat. I peel in the name
of your grandmother, lost
during the deportation.
The skins slap into the sink.
I slice the flesh in the name
of your mother and that SS
officer who saved her
at the embassy gate:
Fräulein, don't go home now,
you wouldn't like the weather.
Oh, you, my love, what a wide river
of blood has washed you here—

JEWISH CEMETERY IN WÜRZBURG, GERMANY

The gravestones were pocked
with algae. Weeds. Grass
                    refused
        to grow. After,
                    flies at the Kaffé
slammed against us,
                    lowered
their gunstock bodies to buzz
                    the croissant on your plate.
        I thought to kill one but was
        too tired. Light fell,
mutable and glinting in code. We
        ordered tea. I touched the tinder
        of your hand.
                    You asked
the starched-pink waitress
            for directions. Amiably
she pointed to the Autobahn,
        hemmed in by commerce.
All afternoon in our rented BMW
                    the fields of rye
                    disheveled
        as we rode those punctual seams.
Tatters. Nothing to be saved.

A MILLION SWAINSON'S THRUSHES

And when the sun closes, they who do
    not know the word for *wings*

leave everything behind—the berries,
    spruce buds and their moths,
        rustling sleeves of beetles.

    Darkly they thrust, pressed past
the past, the stains of stars.

Night-blind, their calls are sequins, bursts of braille.
    In the blind hurtledown, they are

    earth's beloveds,
        shreds of everlasting
            on their diamond backs.

THE COLORADO RIVER

The black water
    snake slithering through

        pickerelweed, bruised fruit
that holds a little sweetness.

    Love the muscle of fleeting—

        the chevron wild geese anchored
to sky, crow, raucous in the pines,

worms that move the earth
    in the field. Yellow toadflax,

        the ditches and gravel pits
where it grows. The hawk

moth—its wings, its velvet hatchets,
    its tongue threading that

        flower's puckered lip down
the long-spurred honey highway.

Love the river for daring
    to leave, the sea for returning.

RIDING BAREBACK

In the territory of best intention, I bend

        with him who whips

the wind. I cling to him

        like a needle in a vinyl groove,

            flecked with sweat, numb

to everything but his plunging hooves,

his four-pronged thunder striking ground,

        trampling ironweed, startling up

            again a flock of starlings—

I let loose the reins, lean forward,

        grip his withers, the cord of his warm neck,

whisper into his chestnut ear, *Keep going.*

        Finish what you've started!

Wendy Drexler grew up in Denver, Colorado, was educated at the University of Pennsylvania, and now lives in Belmont, Massachusetts. Nominated for a Pushcart Prize, her chapbook, *Drive-Ins, Gas Stations, the Bright Motels,* was published by Pudding House in 2007. Her poems have been published in numerous literary journals, including *Barrow Street, Cider Press Review, The Comstock Review, Ibbetson Street, Nimrod* (semifinalist, 2006 Nimrod/Hardman Pablo Neruda Prize), *Off the Coast, Poetry East, RHINO, Tar River Poetry,* and in the anthology *Blood to Remember: American Poets on the Holocaust.* She is a poetry editor for *Sanctuary,* the journal of the Massachusetts Audubon Society, and a freelance writer and editor.

CPSIA information can be obtained at www.ICGtesting.com
Printed in the USA
BVOW021828271212

309190BV00001B/26/P